Enslow PUBLISHING

BY KATHRYN WALTON

VOL. I **From Past to President** 1861

ABRAHAM LINCOLN

Please visit our website, www.enslow.com. For a free color catalog of all our high-quality books, call toll free 1-800-398-2504 or fax 1-877-980-4454.

Library of Congress Cataloging-in-Publication Data

Names: Walton, Kathryn, 1993- author.
Title: Abraham Lincoln / Kathryn Walton.
Description: Buffalo, NY : Enslow Publishing, 2025. | Series: From past to president | Includes bibliographical references and index.
Identifiers: LCCN 2024028834 (print) | LCCN 2024028835 (ebook) | ISBN 9781978542310 (library binding) | ISBN 9781978542303 (paperback) | ISBN 9781978542327 (ebook)
Subjects: LCSH: Lincoln, Abraham, 1809-1865–Juvenile literature. | Presidents–United States–Biography–Juvenile literature. | United States–History–Civil War, 1861-1865–Juvenile literature. | United States–Politics and government–1861-1865–Juvenile literature.
Classification: LCC E457.905 .W345 2025 (print) | LCC E457.905 (ebook) | DDC 973.7092 [B]–dc23/eng/20240801
LC record available at https://lccn.loc.gov/2024028834
LC ebook record available at https://lccn.loc.gov/2024028835

Published in 2025 by
Enslow Publishing
2544 Clinton Street
Buffalo, NY 14224

Copyright © 2025 Enslow Publishing

Portions of this work were originally authored by Gillian Gosman and published as *Abraham Lincoln*. All new material in this edition is authored by Kathryn Walton.

Designer: Claire Zimmermann
Editor: Natalie Humphrey

Photo credits: Cover (Abraham Lincoln, cabin), p. 17 Everett Collection/Shutterstock.com; cover (woods illustration) sar14ev/Shutterstock.com; cover, p. 11 (Lincoln as a lawyer), p. 5 (portrait), p. 13 (map) courtesy of the Library of Congress; cover (newspaper clipping) STILLFX/Shutterstock.com; cover (Abraham Lincoln signature) Abraham_Lincoln_Signature.png/Wikimedia Commons; cover (author name scrap), series art (caption background) Robyn Mackenzie/Shutterstock.com; series art (blue paper background) OLeksiiTooz/Shutterstock.com; cover (newspaper text background at lower left) MaryValery/Shutterstock.com; series art (newspaper text background) TanyaFox/Shutterstock; series art (More to Learn antique tag) Mega Pixel/Shutterstock.com; pp. 5, 9, 11, 19 (ripped blank newspaper piece) STILLFX/Shutterstock.com; p. 7 Last_Home_of_the_Parents_of_Abraham_Lincoln,_Farmington,_Illinois,_Built_1831.png/Wikimedia Commons; p. 9 Internet Archive Book Images/flickr; p. 11 Lincoln_Douglas.jpg/Wikimedia Commons; p. 15 (map) Rainer Lesniewski/Shutterstock.com; p. 15 (map background) Anatoliy Sadovskiy/Shutterstock.com; p. 19 courtesy of New York Public Library; p. 21 (paper scraps) SB Professional/Shutterstock.com.

All rights reserved. No part of this book may be reproduced in any form without permission in writing from the publisher, except by a reviewer.

Some of the images in this book illustrate individuals who are models. The depictions do not imply actual situations or events.

Printed in the United States of America

CPSIA compliance information: Batch #CWENS25: For further information contact Enslow Publishing at 1-800-398-2504.

CONTENTS

President Abraham Lincoln 4
Lincoln's Birth 6
A Young Lincoln 8
Working Hard 10
Lincoln versus Douglas 12
The South Secedes 14
The Civil War 16
Lincoln Speaks 18
Remembering Lincoln 20
President Lincoln's Timeline 21
Glossary 22
For More Information 23
Index 24

Words in the glossary appear in **bold** type the first time they are used in the text.

PRESIDENT ABRAHAM LINCOLN

Not many people could oversee a nation at war with itself, but Abraham Lincoln did! Through his strength, hard work, and **dedication** to his country, Lincoln led the United States through the Civil War.

Before Lincoln ran for office, he was a poor young man from Kentucky. With his love of learning, Lincoln shaped himself into a great speaker, strong leader, and thoughtful man. Many people even say he was one of the greatest presidents!

Abraham Lincoln was 52 when he was elected, or chosen for, president.

MORE TO KNOW

Lincoln became the 16th president of the United States.

LINCOLN'S BIRTH

Abraham Lincoln was born to a family of poor settlers on February 12, 1809. They lived in a one-room cabin in Kentucky. The family moved to Indiana when Lincoln was seven. His mother died two years later.

MORE TO KNOW

Lincoln was always tall as a child and he grew to be taller than most men of his time! He was 6 feet 4 inches (1.9 m) tall.

Young Lincoln loved to learn, but couldn't go to school often. Because his family was poor, Lincoln needed to work instead. He borrowed many books and taught himself in his free time. Lincoln and his family moved to Illinois in 1830.

The log cabin pictured here was the home of Lincoln's family in Farmington, Illinois.

A YOUNG LINCOLN

During Lincoln's youth, the United States was growing quickly. With this growth came disagreement. Southern farmers wanted to own **enslaved** people to work their fields. Many northerners believed that slavery was wrong. They wanted to abolish, or end, slavery.

The government made a **compromise** to keep an even number of slave states and free states. The Missouri Compromise of 1820 allowed slavery in the new state of Missouri and outlawed slavery in the new state of Maine.

The Missouri Compromise also banned slavery in the northern part of the **Louisiana Purchase.**

MORE TO KNOW

The Missouri Compromise affected states added after the Compromise was made. Arkansas was added in 1836 as a slave state. Michigan, a free state, was added in 1837.

WORKING HARD

Lincoln worked moving loads on boats, as a shopkeeper, and even as a postmaster. Later, he took part in local **politics**. In 1834, he was elected to the Illinois General Assembly, part of Illinois's state government.

Lincoln also studied law. He never went to law school. He taught himself to be a **lawyer**. In 1837, he opened his law office in Springfield, Illinois. Lincoln worked hard. His law partner said of Lincoln, "His **ambition** was a little engine that knew no rest."

Lincoln was a lawyer in Springfield, Illinois, for almost 25 years.

MORE TO KNOW

In 1842, Lincoln married Mary Todd. Although they had four sons, only one lived to be an adult.

LINCOLN VERSUS DOUGLAS

Lincoln ran for Congress in 1858. He ran against Stephen A. Douglas. During the race, the two men held debates. Debates are public arguments about ideas. Lincoln and Douglas argued about slavery. Lincoln spoke against slavery, while Douglas spoke in favor of it.

MORE TO KNOW

The debates between Abraham Lincoln and Stephen Douglas became well-known across the nation. These seven debates were later known as the Lincoln-Douglas debates.

Lincoln lost the election, but the debates made him widely known. In 1860, he was chosen as the Republican **candidate** for president of the United States.

Lincoln's antislavery message during the Lincoln-Douglas debates made him unpopular in the South.

THE SOUTH SECEDES

Even though most Southern states didn't vote for him, Lincoln still won the election of 1860. After Lincoln was elected president, seven southern states **seceded** from the United States. They formed the Confederate States of America, also called the Confederacy. The northern states were called the Union.

On April 12, 1861, Confederate troops opened fire on Fort Sumter in South Carolina. This battle marked the beginning of the Civil War. The Confederacy won. Soon after, four more states joined the Confederacy.

THE UNITED STATES IN 1861

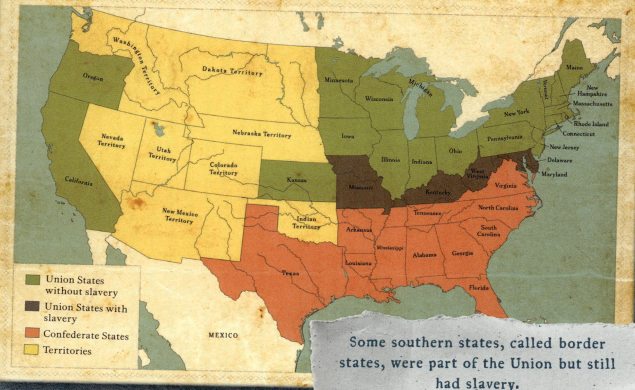

Some southern states, called border states, were part of the Union but still had slavery.

MORE TO KNOW

The Confederate states were South Carolina, Mississippi, Florida, Alabama, Georgia, Louisiana, Texas, Virginia, Arkansas, Tennessee, and North Carolina.

THE CIVIL WAR

During the Civil War, Lincoln had to make many hard decisions. The Union lost to the Confederacy in many battles and didn't have enough soldiers to keep fighting. Lincoln created a **draft** to force people in the Union to fight in the war. He also warned the Confederacy that if it kept fighting, all the enslaved people in the Confederacy would be freed.

True to his word, on January 1, 1863, Lincoln freed the enslaved people of the Confederacy with the Emancipation Proclamation.

MORE TO KNOW

The Emancipation Proclamation didn't free enslaved people across the country. It did not free enslaved people in border states.

Many freed enslaved people joined the Union army to help fight in the war.

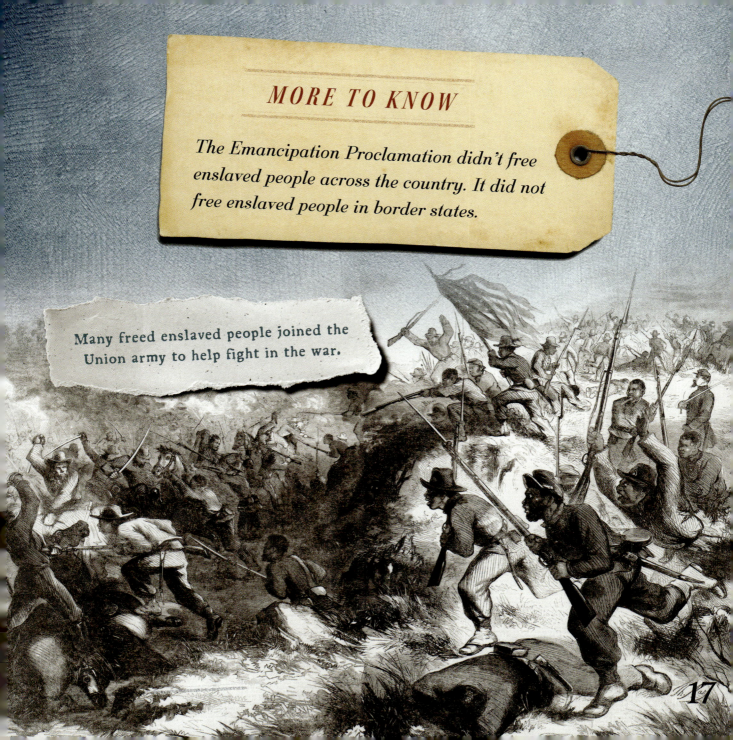

17

LINCOLN SPEAKS

Lincoln was a powerful speaker. Several months after the Union victory at Gettysburg in Pennsylvania, Lincoln gave a speech near the battlefield. This famous speech was the Gettysburg Address. It was Lincoln's promise to create an America that was free for all.

In 1864, Lincoln was reelected, and in 1865, he gave another speech. He said that the Confederate states should not be punished when they rejoined the United States. He said that the nation would be stronger when it was once again working together.

On April 9, 1865, Confederate general Robert E. Lee **surrendered** to Union general Ulysses S. Grant.

MORE TO KNOW

The Gettysburg Address was given to honor the Union soldiers who died during the Battle at Gettysburg.

REMEMBERING LINCOLN

While the Civil War had ended, there was still work to be done to free enslaved people. But Lincoln would not live to see an end to slavery in the United States. On April 14, 1865, John Wilkes Booth shot Lincoln at Ford's Theatre in Washington, DC. Lincoln died the next morning.

President Lincoln is remembered for his work in helping to end slavery and for leading the nation through the Civil War. Lincoln's love of his country, learning, and his fairness guided him through his presidency.

PRESIDENT LINCOLN'S TIMELINE

FEBRUARY 12, 1809
Abraham Lincoln is born in Kentucky.

1830
Lincoln moves to Illinois with his family.

1860
Lincoln is elected the 16th president of the United States.

APRIL 12, 1861
The Battle of Fort Sumter begins the Civil War.

JANUARY 1, 1863
The Emancipation Proclamation frees all enslaved people in the Confederacy.

NOVEMBER 19, 1863
Abraham Lincoln gives the Gettysburg Address in Gettysburg, Pennsylvania.

1864
Lincoln is reelected president of the United States.

APRIL 9, 1865
The Confederate forces surrender to Union forces.

APRIL 14, 1865
Lincoln is shot at Ford's Theatre by John Wilkes Booth.

APRIL 15, 1865
Lincoln dies at 7:22 a.m.

GLOSSARY

ambition: Drive or dedication towards a goal.

candidate: A person who runs in an election.

compromise: A way of two sides reaching agreement in which each gives up something to end an argument.

dedication: Special faithfulness to a cause, place, or thing.

draft: A system that requires young people to serve for a time in their country's armed forces.

enslaved: Having to do with being owned by another person and forced to work without pay.

lawyer: Someone whose job it is to help people with their questions and problems with the law.

Louisiana Purchase: Territory of the western United States bought from France in 1803.

politics: The activities of the government and government officials.

secede: To leave a country.

surrender: To give up.

FOR MORE INFORMATION

BOOKS

Koestler-Grack, Rachel A. *Abraham Lincoln*. Minneapolis, MN: Bellwether Media, 2022.

London, Martha. *Abraham Lincoln*. Lake Elmo, MN: Focus Readers, 2023.

WEBSITES

Britannica Kids: Abraham Lincoln
https://kids.britannica.com/kids/article/Abraham-Lincoln/345491
Check out photographs and learn more about Abraham Lincoln.

National Geographic Kids: Abraham Lincoln
www.kids.nationalgeographic.com/history/article/abraham-lincoln
Learn more about Abraham Lincoln's time in office and the work he did during the Civil War.

Publisher's note to educators and parents: Our editors have carefully reviewed these websites to ensure that they are suitable for students. Many websites change frequently, however, and we cannot guarantee that a site's future contents will continue to meet our high standards of quality and educational value. Be advised that students should be closely supervised whenever they access the internet.

INDEX

battles, 14, 16, 18, 19, 21
Booth, John Wilkes, 20, 21
border states, 15, 17
Confederacy, 14, 16, 17, 21
Congress, 12
debates, 12, 13
Douglas, Stephen A., 12, 13
Emancipation Proclamation, 16, 17, 21
Ford's Theatre, 20
Fort Sumter, 14, 21
Gettysburg Address, 18, 19, 21
Grant, Ulysses S., 19
height, 6

Illinois, 7, 10, 11, 21
Indiana, 6
Kentucky, 4, 6, 21
law, 10
Lee, Robert E., 15
Missouri Compromise, 8, 9
mother, 6
postmaster, 10
school, 7, 10
slavery, 8, 9, 12, 15, 20
state government, 10
Todd, Mary, 11
Union, 14, 15, 16, 17, 18, 19, 21